Your
BEAUTY &
LOVE CHASE AFTER ME
EVERY DAY OF MY LIFE.
PSALM 23:6 MSG

FOR WE KNOW HOW DEARLY
GOD LOVES US, BECAUSE
HE HAS GIVEN US THE
HOLY SPIRIT TO FILL OUR
HEARTS WITH HIS LOVE.

ROMANS 5:5 NLT

Because you belong to Christ Jesus, God's peace will stand **guard** over all your thoughts and feelings. His peace can do this far better than our human minds.

Philippians 4:7 ERV

NOTHING
IN ALL CREATION
WILL EVER BE ABLE
TO SEPARATE US FROM
THE LOVE OF GOD
THAT IS REVEALED IN
CHRIST JESUS
OUR LORD.
ROMANS 8:39 NLT

I CAN DO ALL THINGS
THROUGH CHRIST
BECAUSE HE GIVES ME
STRENGTH.
PHILIPPIANS 4:13 ICB

"REMEMBER, I COMMANDED YOU TO BE STRONG & BRAVE. DON'T BE AFRAID, BECAUSE THE LORD YOUR GOD WILL BE WITH YOU WHEREVER YOU GO."
JOSHUA 1:9 ERV

THE LORD'S
DELIGHT
IS IN THOSE
WHO FEAR HIM,
THOSE WHO PUT
THEIR HOPE
IN HIS UNFAILING
LOVE.
PSALM 147:11 NLT

AND WE KNOW
THAT IN ALL THINGS
GOD WORKS FOR THE
GOOD OF THOSE
WHO LOVE HIM, WHO
HAVE BEEN CALLED
ACCORDING TO HIS
PURPOSE.
ROMANS 8:28 NIV

WE HOPE IN THE
LIVING GOD WHO IS THE
SAVIOR OF ALL PEOPLE,
ESPECIALLY OF THOSE
WHO BELIEVE.
1 TIMOTHY 4:10 NCV

AFTER YOU HAVE SUFFERED FOR A LITTLE WHILE, THE GOD OF ALL GRACE, WHO HAS CALLED US TO HIS **ETERNAL GLORY** THROUGH CHRIST JESUS, WILL RESTORE, SUPPORT, **STRENGTHEN**, AND ESTABLISH YOU.

1 PETER 5:10 MEV

"COME TO ME,
ALL OF YOU WHO ARE TIRED
AND HAVE HEAVY LOADS,
AND I WILL GIVE YOU REST."

MATTHEW 11:28 NCV

Those
who hope
in the Lord
will renew
their strength.
They will soar on
wings like eagles;
they will run and
not grow weary,
they will walk
and not be faint.

Isaiah 40:31 NIV

"MY GRACE IS ALL YOU NEED. MY POWER WORKS BEST IN WEAKNESS." SO NOW I AM GLAD TO BOAST ABOUT MY WEAKNESSES, SO THAT THE POWER OF CHRIST CAN WORK THROUGH ME.

2 CORINTHIANS 12:9 NLT

HE WHO TRUSTS IN THE LORD,
LOVINGKINDNESS SHALL SURROUND HIM.

PSALM 32:10 NASB

HE LOVES WHATEVER
IS JUST AND GOOD;
THE EARTH IS FILLED
WITH HIS TENDER LOVE.

PSALM 33:5 TLB

THE LORD IS NEAR
TO THE BROKENHEARTED AND
SAVES THOSE WHO ARE CRUSHED IN
SPIRIT. MANY ARE THE AFFLICTIONS
OF THE RIGHTEOUS, BUT THE LORD
DELIVERS HIM OUT OF THEM ALL.

PSALM 34:18–19 NASB

TRUST IN THE LORD WITH ALL YOUR **HEART**
AND DO NOT LEAN ON YOUR OWN UNDERSTANDING.
IN **ALL** YOUR **WAYS** ACKNOWLEDGE HIM,
AND HE WILL MAKE YOUR PATHS STRAIGHT.

PROVERBS 3:5-6 NASB

IF YOU CONFESS WITH YOUR MOUTH THE LORD JESUS AND BELIEVE IN YOUR HEART THAT GOD HAS RAISED HIM FROM THE DEAD, YOU WILL BE SAVED.

ROMANS 10:9 NKJV

"ALL OF YOU,
TAKE UP MY YOKE AND
LEARN FROM ME, BECAUSE I AM
GENTLE AND HUMBLE
IN HEART, AND YOU
WILL FIND REST
FOR YOURSELVES."
MATTHEW 11:29 HCSB

For God so **loved** the world, that he gave his only Son, that whoever believes in him should not perish but have eternal life.

John 3:16 ESV

DELIGHT
YOURSELF IN THE
LORD, AND HE WILL
GIVE YOU THE DESIRES
OF YOUR HEART.
PSALM 37:4 ISV

"DO NOT FEAR,
FOR I AM WITH YOU; DO
NOT ANXIOUSLY LOOK ABOUT
YOU, FOR I AM YOUR GOD.
I WILL STRENGTHEN
YOU, SURELY I WILL HELP
YOU, SURELY I WILL
UPHOLD YOU WITH MY
RIGHTEOUS RIGHT HAND."

ISAIAH 41:10 NASB

THE EYE OF THE LORD
IS ON THOSE WHO FEAR HIM,
ON THOSE WHO HOPE IN
HIS STEADFAST
LOVE.

PSALM 33:18 ESV

ADMIT YOUR FAULTS TO ONE ANOTHER AND PRAY FOR EACH OTHER SO THAT YOU MAY BE HEALED. THE EARNEST PRAYER OF A RIGHTEOUS MAN HAS GREAT POWER AND WONDERFUL RESULTS.
JAMES 5:16 TLB

"I WILL BE WITH YOU ALWAYS, EVEN UNTIL THE END OF THIS AGE."

MATTHEW 28:20 NCV

AND MY GOD WILL SUPPLY EVERY NEED OF YOURS ACCORDING TO HIS RICHES IN GLORY IN CHRIST JESUS.

PHILIPPIANS 4:19 ESV

For by grace
YOU HAVE BEEN SAVED
THROUGH FAITH, AND
THAT NOT OF YOURSELVES;
IT IS THE GIFT OF GOD.
EPHESIANS 2:8 NKJV

"For I know the PLANS
I have for you," declares the Lord,
"plans to PROSPER you and not to harm you,
plans to give you HOPE and a FUTURE."

Jeremiah 29: 11 NIV

BECAUSE OF
HIS GREAT LOVE FOR US,
GOD, WHO IS RICH IN MERCY,
MADE US **ALIVE WITH CHRIST**
EVEN WHEN WE WERE DEAD IN
TRANSGRESSIONS—IT IS BY GRACE
YOU HAVE BEEN SAVED.
EPHESIANS 2:4–5 NIV

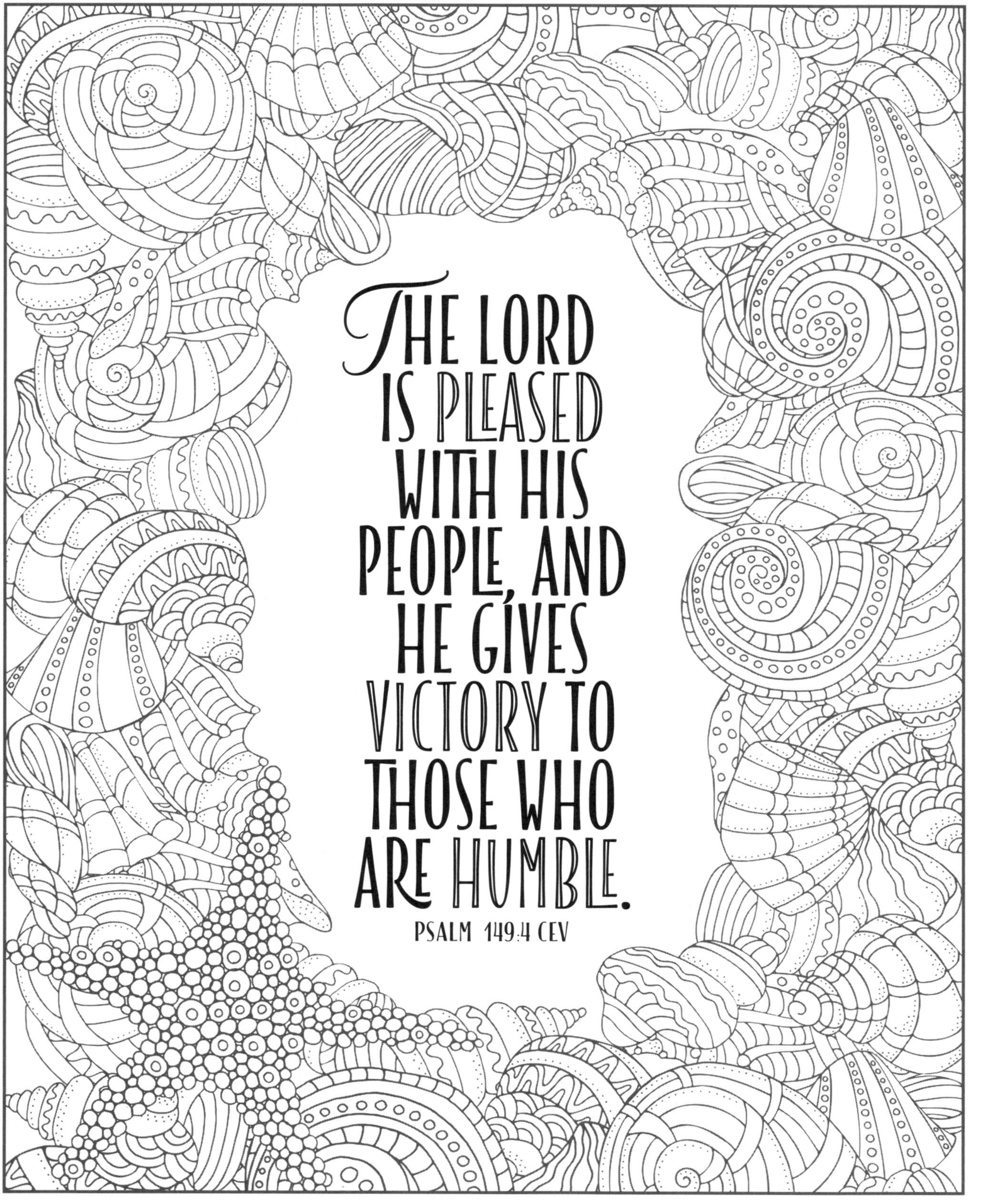

THE LORD IS PLEASED WITH HIS PEOPLE, AND HE GIVES VICTORY TO THOSE WHO ARE HUMBLE.

PSALM 149:4 CEV

Hope
DOES NOT PUT US TO SHAME,
BECAUSE GOD'S LOVE HAS BEEN
POURED INTO OUR HEARTS
THROUGH THE HOLY SPIRIT
WHO HAS BEEN GIVEN TO US.
ROMANS 5:5 ESV

I AM CONFIDENT OF THIS VERY THING,
THAT HE WHO BEGAN A GOOD WORK
IN YOU WILL PERFECT IT UNTIL
THE DAY OF JESUS CHRIST.

PHILIPPIANS 1:6 MEV

THE FRUIT
OF THE SPIRIT
IS LOVE, JOY,
PEACE, PATIENCE,
KINDNESS,
GOODNESS,
FAITHFULNESS,
GENTLENESS,
SELF-CONTROL;
AGAINST SUCH THINGS
THERE IS NO LAW.

GALATIANS 5:22–23 NASB

"May the Lord
bless and protect you;
may the Lord's face radiate
with joy because of you;
may he be gracious to you,
show you his favor, and
give you his peace."

Numbers 6:24–26 TLB

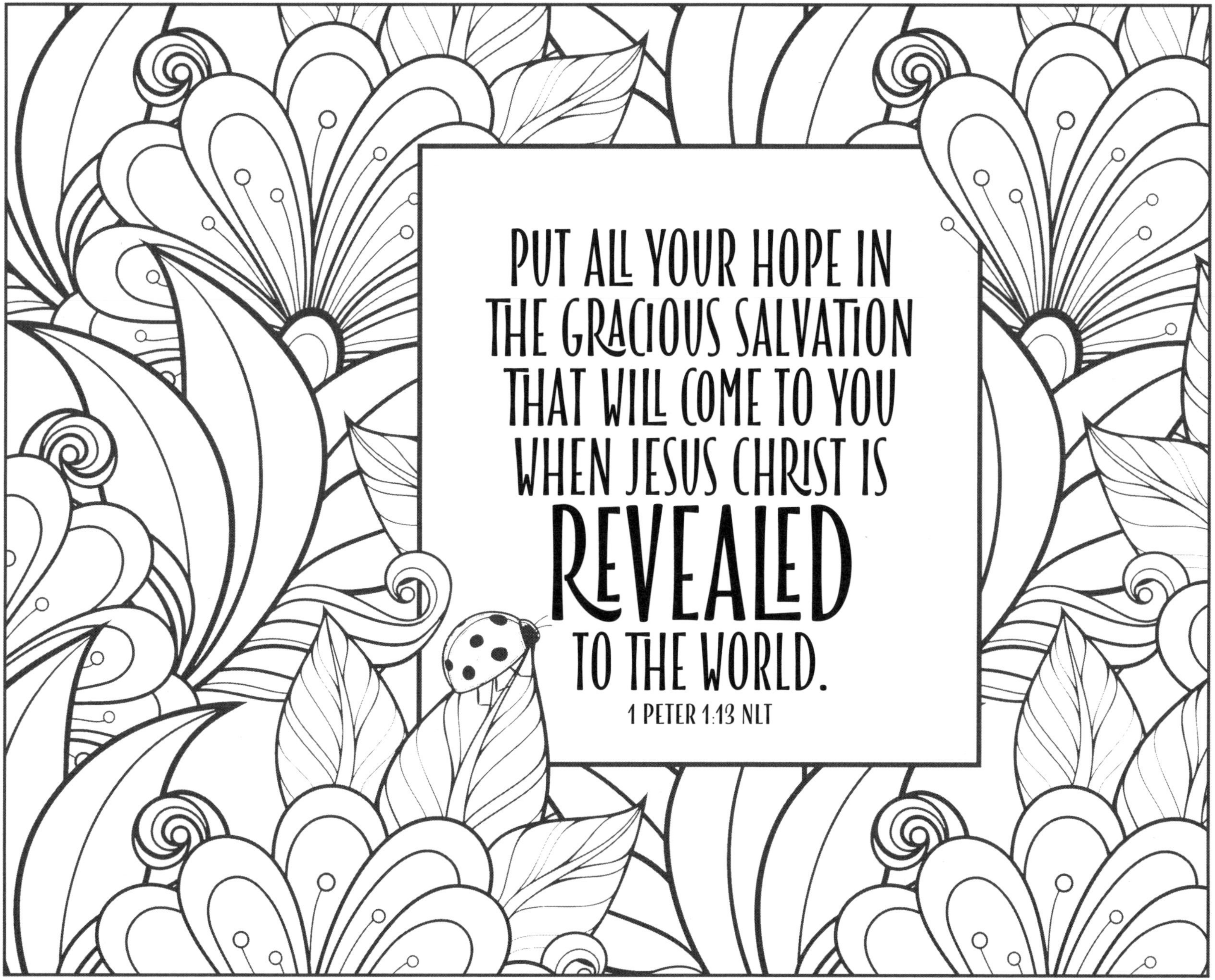
PUT ALL YOUR HOPE IN
THE GRACIOUS SALVATION
THAT WILL COME TO YOU
WHEN JESUS CHRIST IS
REVEALED
TO THE WORLD.
1 PETER 1:13 NLT

BUT IF ANY OF YOU LACKS WISDOM,
LET HIM ASK OF GOD, WHO GIVES TO ALL
GENEROUSLY AND WITHOUT REPROACH,
AND IT WILL BE GIVEN TO HIM.
JAMES 1:5 NASB

"NO EYE HAS SEEN,
NO EAR HAS HEARD,
AND NO MIND HAS IMAGINED
WHAT **GOD** HAS PREPARED
FOR THOSE WHO LOVE HIM."

1 CORINTHIANS 2:9 NLT

GRACE, MERCY
AND PEACE
FROM GOD THE FATHER
AND FROM JESUS CHRIST,
THE FATHER'S SON,
WILL BE WITH US IN
TRUTH AND
LOVE.
2 JOHN 1:3 NIV

HE LETS ME **REST** IN THE MEADOW GRASS AND LEADS ME BESIDE THE QUIET STREAMS. HE GIVES ME NEW **STRENGTH**. HE HELPS ME DO WHAT HONORS HIM THE MOST.

PSALM 23:2-3 TLB

I pray
that the eyes of your HEART
may be enlightened in order that you may know
the HOPE to which he has called you.
EPHESIANS 1:18 NIV

Our Lord
AND OUR GOD, YOU ARE LIKE
THE SUN AND ALSO LIKE A SHIELD.
YOU TREAT US WITH KINDNESS
AND WITH HONOR, NEVER
DENYING ANY GOOD THING TO
THOSE WHO LIVE RIGHT.
PSALM 84:11 CEV

BE STRONG AND COURAGEOUS,

ALL YOU WHO PUT YOUR HOPE IN THE LORD!

PSALM 31:24 NLT

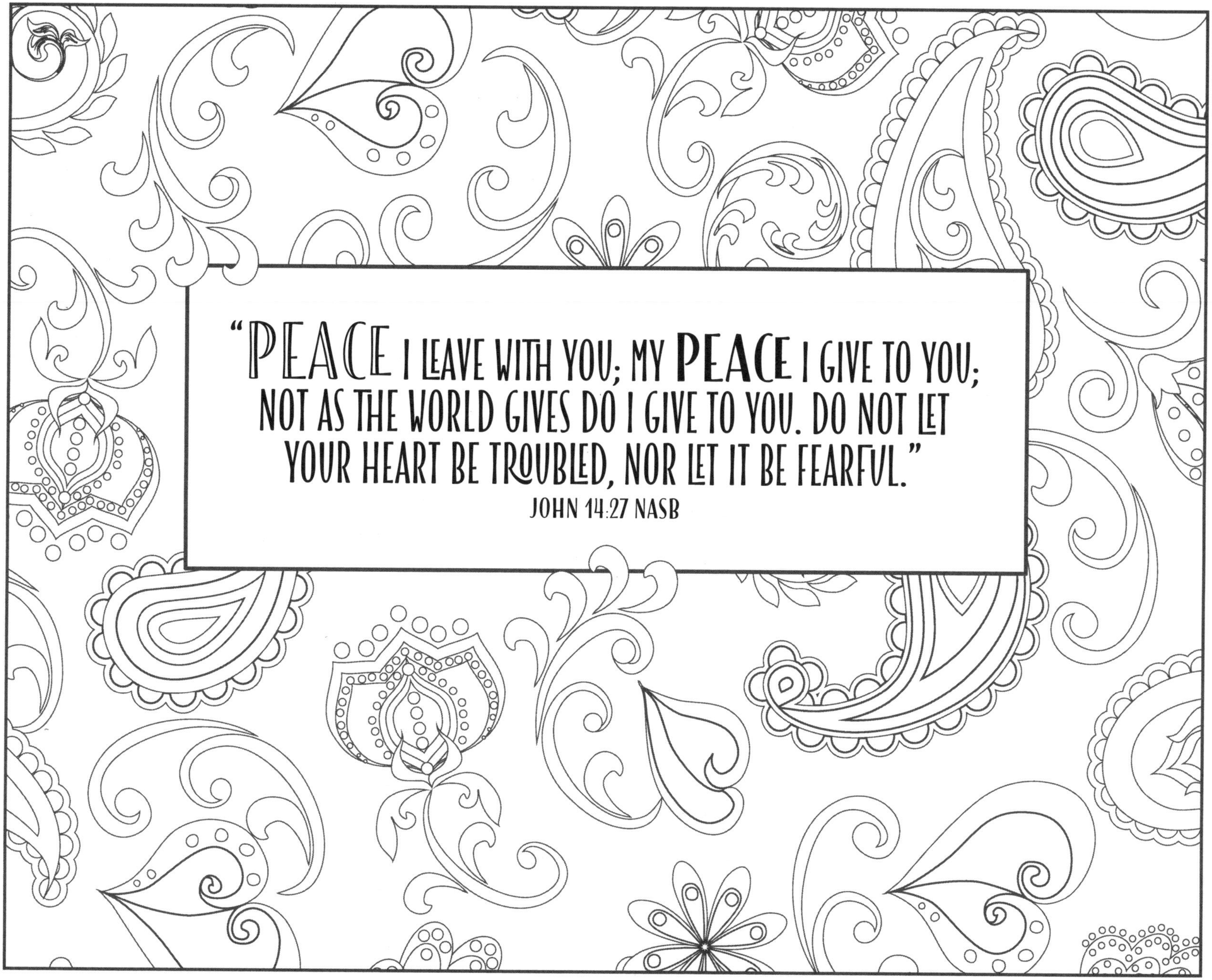
"PEACE I LEAVE WITH YOU; MY PEACE I GIVE TO YOU; NOT AS THE WORLD GIVES DO I GIVE TO YOU. DO NOT LET YOUR HEART BE TROUBLED, NOR LET IT BE FEARFUL."
JOHN 14:27 NASB

HOPE
IN THE LORD,
AND KEEP HIS WAY,
AND HE WILL EXALT YOU
TO INHERIT THE LAND.
PSALM 37:34 MEV

LET HIM HAVE ALL YOUR WORRIES AND CARES,
FOR HE IS ALWAYS **THINKING** ABOUT YOU AND
WATCHING **EVERYTHING** THAT CONCERNS YOU.

1 PETER 5:7 TLB

You are my
hiding place
& my shield;
I hope in
your word.
PSALM 119:114 ESV

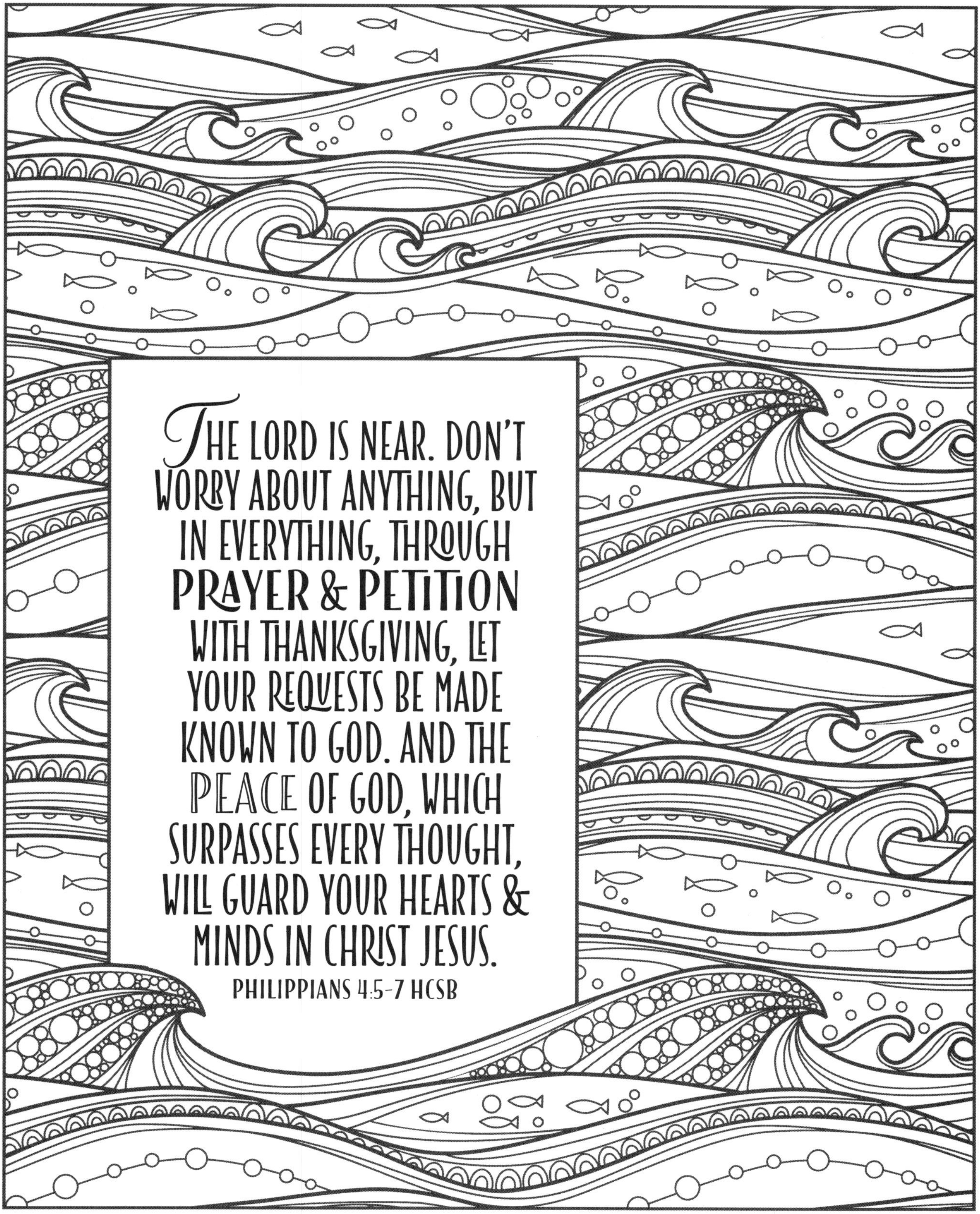

The Lord is near. Don't worry about anything, but in everything, through **prayer & petition** with thanksgiving, let your requests be made known to God. And the peace of God, which surpasses every thought, will guard your hearts & minds in Christ Jesus.

Philippians 4:5-7 HCSB

Now may our
Lord Jesus Christ himself
and God our Father,
who loved us and by grace
gave us eternal comfort
and good hope, encourage
your hearts and strengthen
you in every good thing
you do or say.
2 Thessalonians
2:16–17 NET